A DK PUBLISHING BOOK

Editor Lara Tankel Holtz
Designer Helen Melville
Managing Editor Sheila Hanly
US Editor Camela Decaire
Production Catherine Semark
Illustrator Ellis Nadler
Photography Mike Dunning
Additional photography
Finbar Hawkins, Ray Moller
Consultant John Poulter

First American Edition, 1995
2 4 6 8 10 9 7 5 3

Published in the United States by
DK Publishing, Inc
95 Madison Avenue, New York, New York 10016

Library of Congress Cataloging-in-Publication Data
Llewellyn, Claire.
Tractor / Claire Llewellyn. – 1st American ed.   p. cm.
ISBN 1-56458-515-8
1. Agricultural machinery--Juvenile literature. 2. Farm tractors--
Juvenile literature. (1. Tractors. 2. Agricultural machinery . 3.
Machinery.) I. Title
S675.25.L58 1995
631.3'7--dc20   94-24403
CIP
AC

Color reproduction by Chromagraphics, Singapore
Printed in Italy by L.E.G.O.

Dorling Kindersley would like to thank
Goughs of Hunsingore, Greenland UK Ltd.,
and Duncan Chapman for their
help in producing this book.

The publisher would like to thank the
following for their kind permission to
reproduce photographs: Greenland UK Ltd.:
14, 20 top center World Pictures,
Feature Pix Colour Library Ltd.: 15 bottom right

Scale
Look out for drawings like
this – they show the size
of machines compared
with people.

Combine harvester
Page 12

Forage harvester
Page 15

Baler
Page 17

Farm loader
Page 18

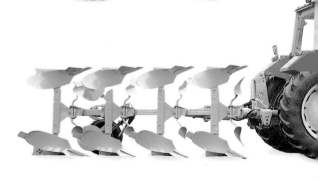

Trailer
Page 20

Plow
Page 9

Mighty Machines

TRACTOR

Claire Llewellyn

Manure spreader
Page 11

Tractor
Page 6

DK

Tractor

A tractor is the most important machine on a farm. Its powerful engine helps it pull along other machinery to do different jobs. Its large wheels stop it from getting stuck in any mud.

cab

7110   CASE INT

small front wheels swivel to turn the tractor

big tires help the tractor roll smoothly over bumps

ridges on the tires grip even slippery mud

A **tire** is a rubber ring fitted around a wheel and filled with air.

Hitched up

At the back of a tractor are three hitches. Other farm machines can be hooked onto these.

hitches are controlled by levers in the cab

AMAZING FACTS

Some tractors have a carpet, stereo, and even a cooler to keep the driver happy.

The powerful tractor engine has the same pulling power of at least 200 horses.

A tractor weighs up to 7 tons (6 tonnes) – that's as heavy as 250 seven-year-old children.

Scale

headlight is turned on when driving at night

The driver sits in the **cab**, which contains the steering wheel and controls.

Preparing the soil

Farmers use a tractor and plow to cut and turn soil before planting a crop. A plow's steel blades dig deep into the soil and turn it over, leaving long grooves called furrows.

Scale

Racehorses can run a 4 mile (6.5 km) race in 3 minutes. It would take a tractor and plow 25 minutes to go the same distance.

Some plows weigh 2 tons (2 tonnes) – as much as two small cars.

cab is high up so the driver can see all around

8   A **blade** is a sharp edge usually used for cutting.   **Steel** is a hard, tough metal.

steel blades of the
power harrow cut
through lumps
of soil

Smoothing the bumps
The ground is very rough
after plowing. A furrow press
smooths the bumpy soil and
a power harrow breaks up
the lumps.

furrow press

Horsepower (hp)
Before the tractor was
invented, plows were
pulled by horses. This
tractor has the pulling
power of 170 horses.
It is said to have a
170 hp engine.

blades turn
over soil

plow is hooked
to the back of
the tractor

Horsepower (hp) is the unit used to measure the strength of an engine.

Planting the crop

A seed drill can sow a 30 acre (12 hectare) field in one day. It would take one person at least a week to do the same thing.

Scale

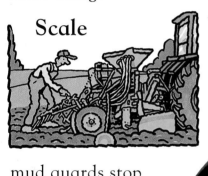

mud guards stop mud from flying into the machine

When a field is ready for planting, a farmer pours seeds into a seed drill. The drill's hollow blades dig holes in the ground. The seeds drop through the blades into the holes, and then rods fill them with dirt.

grooves in tractor tires are 2 inches (5cm) deep

10　Seeds grow on plants. After they are sown in the ground, they grow into new plants.

Manure spreader

A manure spreader spreads manure over a field. Manure feeds the soil, helping plants grow healthily.

seeds are blown down tubes by a stream of air

the hopper contains seeds

Mucking about

Inside a manure spreader are fast-moving chains. They fling out manure as the machine moves along.

A **drill** is a tool for making holes. **Manure** is the waste matter of animals. 11

Harvesting the crop

A combine harvester does several jobs at once. It harvests, or cuts and gathers, a grain crop. It separates the grain from the straw and places the grain safely in a grain tank. The straw is left in rows on the field to be collected later.

flashing light tells other vehicles to look out

Scale

Combined effort

In the huge wheatfields of Canada and the United States, teams of combines work together to harvest a single field.

big window gives a farmer a clear view of the cutter bar

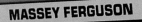

MASSEY FERGUSON

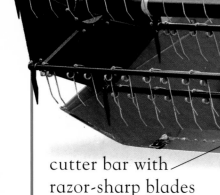

cutter bar with razor-sharp blades

The **grain** is the small, hard seed of a cereal plant such as wheat.

Threshing the crop

In the threshing cylinder, the freshly cut crop is threshed, or shaken, until the grain drops off the stalk.

grain tank

threshing cylinder

funnel can move up and down

a tank of grain pours out of the funnel in less than two minutes

MASSEY FERGUSON

AMAZING FACTS

The grain tank holds 13,250 pounds (6,000kg) of grain – enough to make 7,400 loaves of bread.

A combine can cut a strip over 21 feet (6.5 meters) wide – it would take 16 lawn mowers to cut the same width.

Straw is a plant's stalk. A **cylinder** is a hollow container shaped like a soup can. 13

Harvesting the forage

Crops that farmers feed to their animals in winter, such as grass, are called forage. The grass for forage is cut by a mower. Inside the mower, the grass is squashed between rollers to squeeze out any water. It is then left to dry in the Sun.

swath

After grass has been mowed, it is left in neat bands called **swaths**.

shredded grass
is blown out
of the funnel

Forage harvester

When the mown grass
is dry and wilted, farmers
pick it up with a forage
harvester. This has a
pick-up bar that lifts the
grass into the blades
for chopping.

pick-up
bar

AMAZING FACTS

🔩 The pick-up bar has
24 blades. Each rotates
1,000 times a minute,
cutting and chopping
everything in its path.

🔩 A mower is 10.5 feet
(3.2 meters) wide –
that's as wide as 8 lawn
mowers side by side.

🔩 A forage harvester's
engine is as powerful
as 400 horses.

Harvesting rice

Rice is grown in a flooded field called a paddy
field. A rice harvester chops down the rice plants
and collects the grains in a storage box. A rice
harvester is small and compact so that it does not
sink in the soft paddy fields.

〰️ A **funnel** is a tube that is used to move things from one container to another. 〰️ 15

Hay making

⬡ A hay bale weighs up to 700lb (300kg) – it would take five tough football players to lift it.

⬡ A baler can tie up a bale with twine or netting in 10 seconds.

gases from the engine are cleaned by this filter

Hay is fed to animals in the winter. It is made from the grass that farmers have left to dry in the fields. A hay rake is used to flick and turn over the hay. When the hay is bone dry, it can be gathered and made into bales.

Scale

exhaust pipe

699   MASSEY FERGUSON

steps help farmer up to tractor cab

Gases from the engine are forced out through the **exhaust pipe.**

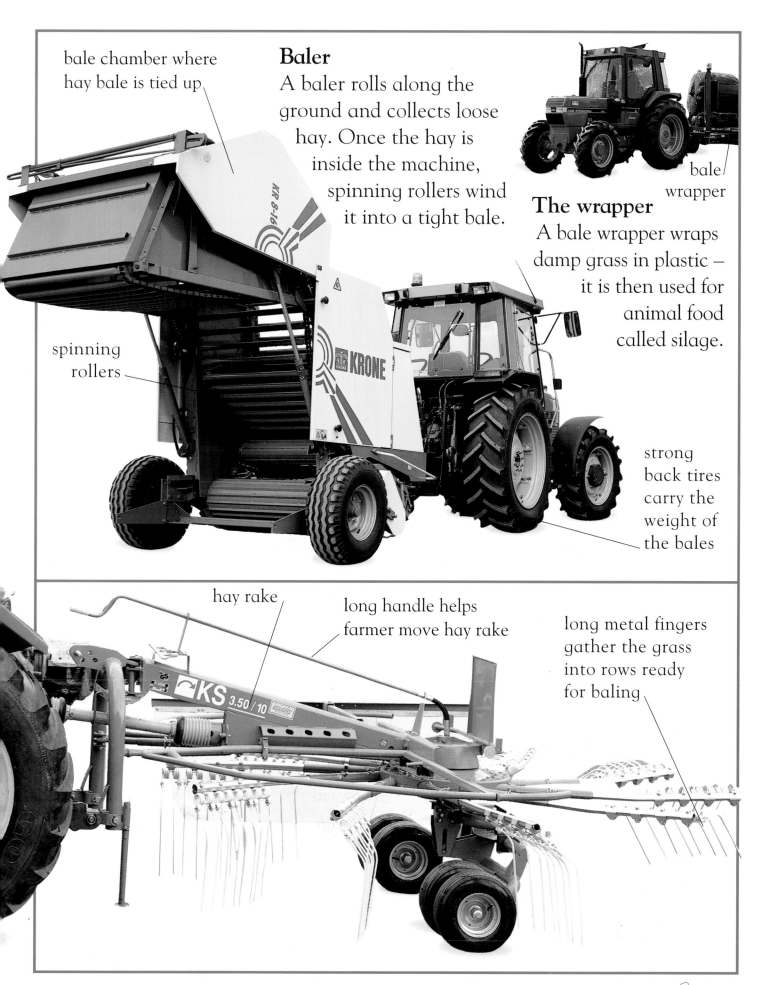

bale chamber where
hay bale is tied up

Baler
A baler rolls along the
ground and collects loose
hay. Once the hay is
inside the machine,
spinning rollers wind
it into a tight bale.

bale
wrapper

The wrapper
A bale wrapper wraps
damp grass in plastic –
it is then used for
animal food
called silage.

spinning
rollers

KRONE

strong
back tires
carry the
weight of
the bales

hay rake

long handle helps
farmer move hay rake

long metal fingers
gather the grass
into rows ready
for baling

KS 3.50 / 10

A **hay bale** is a round or square tightly-packed bundle of hay tied up with string. 17

Lifting and carrying

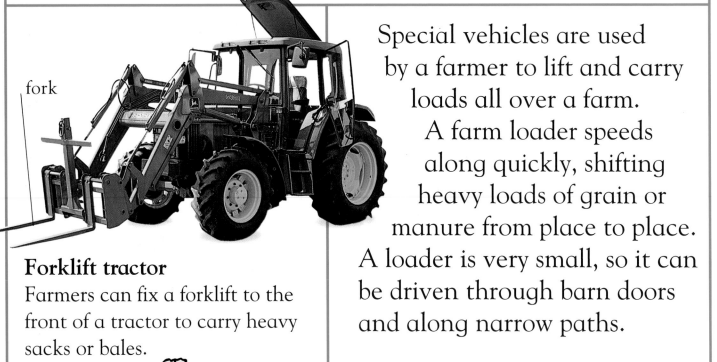

fork

Forklift tractor

Farmers can fix a forklift to the front of a tractor to carry heavy sacks or bales.

Scale

Special vehicles are used by a farmer to lift and carry loads all over a farm.
A farm loader speeds along quickly, shifting heavy loads of grain or manure from place to place.
A loader is very small, so it can be driven through barn doors and along narrow paths.

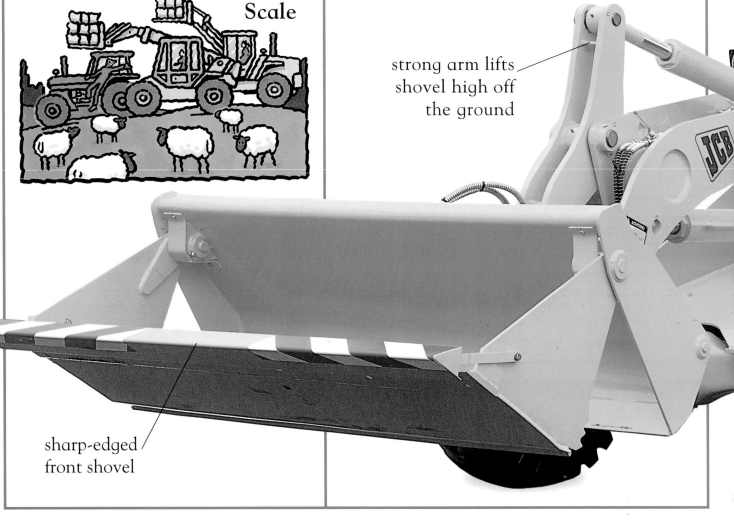

strong arm lifts shovel high off the ground

sharp-edged front shovel

Forks are long prongs that slide under a load and lift it off the ground.

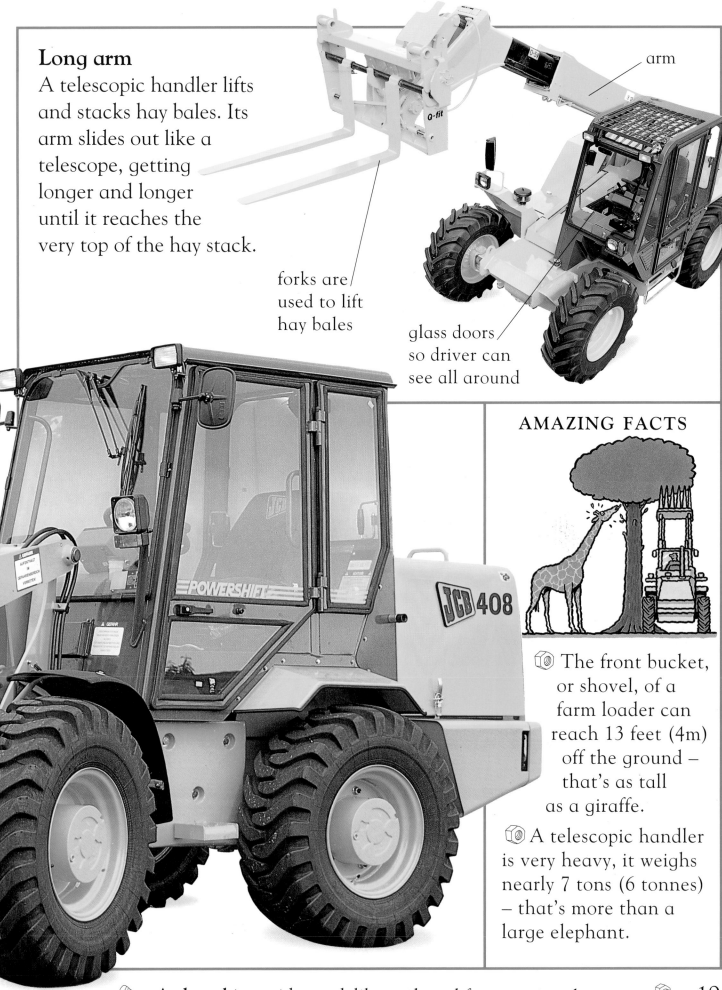

Long arm

A telescopic handler lifts and stacks hay bales. Its arm slides out like a telescope, getting longer and longer until it reaches the very top of the hay stack.

arm

forks are used to lift hay bales

glass doors so driver can see all around

JCB 408

POWERSHIFT

AMAZING FACTS

The front bucket, or shovel, of a farm loader can reach 13 feet (4m) off the ground – that's as tall as a giraffe.

A telescopic handler is very heavy, it weighs nearly 7 tons (6 tonnes) – that's more than a large elephant.

A **shovel** is a wide spadelike tool used for scooping things up. 19

Loading up

The longest trailers are 25 feet (8m) long – big enough to hold a 15-person brass band and all their instruments!

This trailer carries 18 tons (16 tonnes) – more than three elephants.

For moving big and awkward loads, a farmer uses a variety of vehicles. A trailer hitched to the back of a tractor is used to move loose grain from a field to a storage area. Pistons raise up one end of the trailer so it can empty its heavy load.

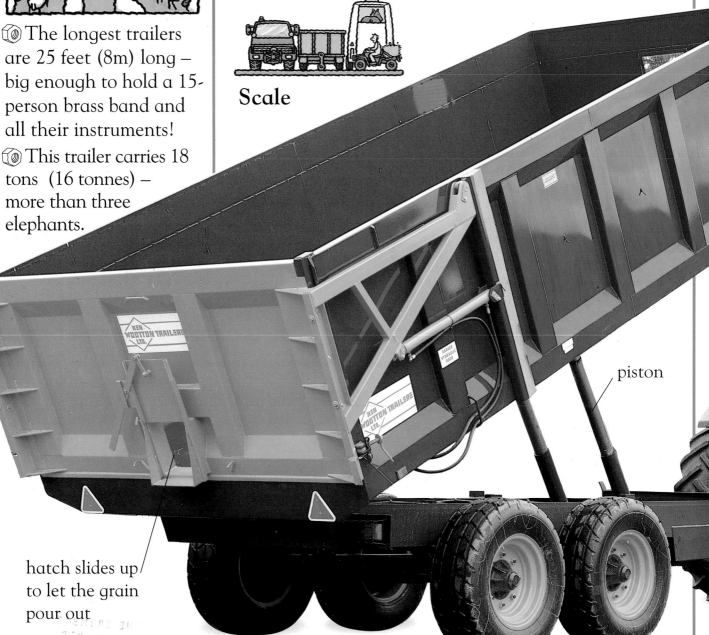

Scale

piston

hatch slides up to let the grain pour out

A **piston** is a metal tube that fits inside a bigger tube and slides in and out.

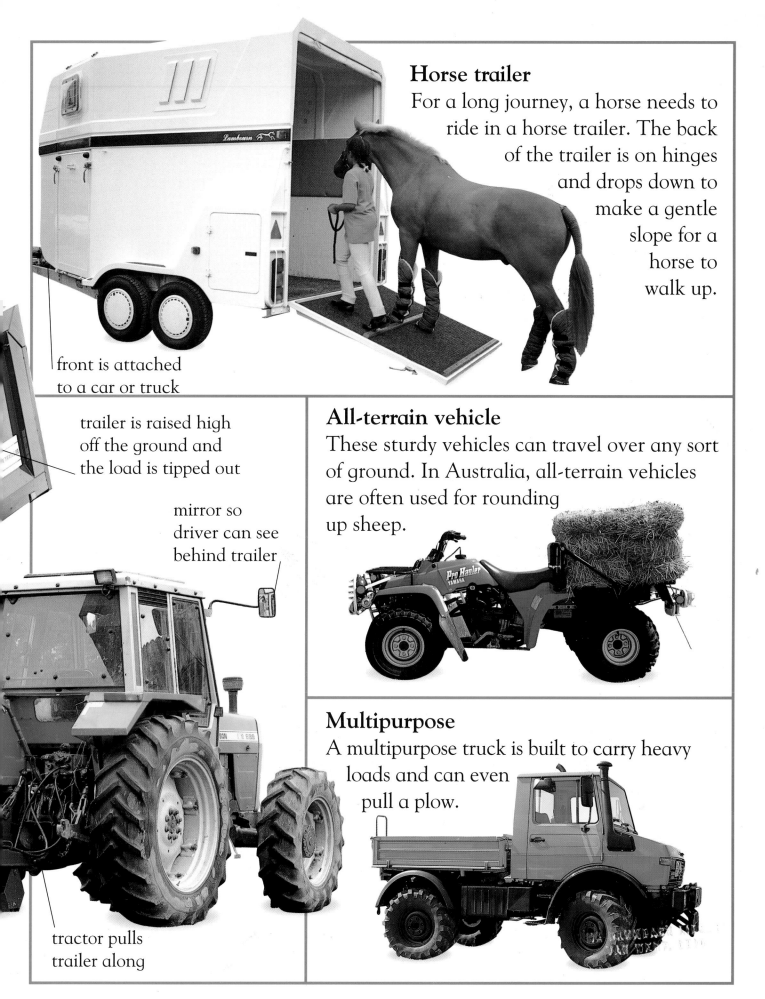

Horse trailer

For a long journey, a horse needs to ride in a horse trailer. The back of the trailer is on hinges and drops down to make a gentle slope for a horse to walk up.

front is attached to a car or truck

trailer is raised high off the ground and the load is tipped out

mirror so driver can see behind trailer

All-terrain vehicle

These sturdy vehicles can travel over any sort of ground. In Australia, all-terrain vehicles are often used for rounding up sheep.

Multipurpose

A multipurpose truck is built to carry heavy loads and can even pull a plow.

tractor pulls trailer along

Terrain is any type of ground – from rocky mountains to sandy deserts.

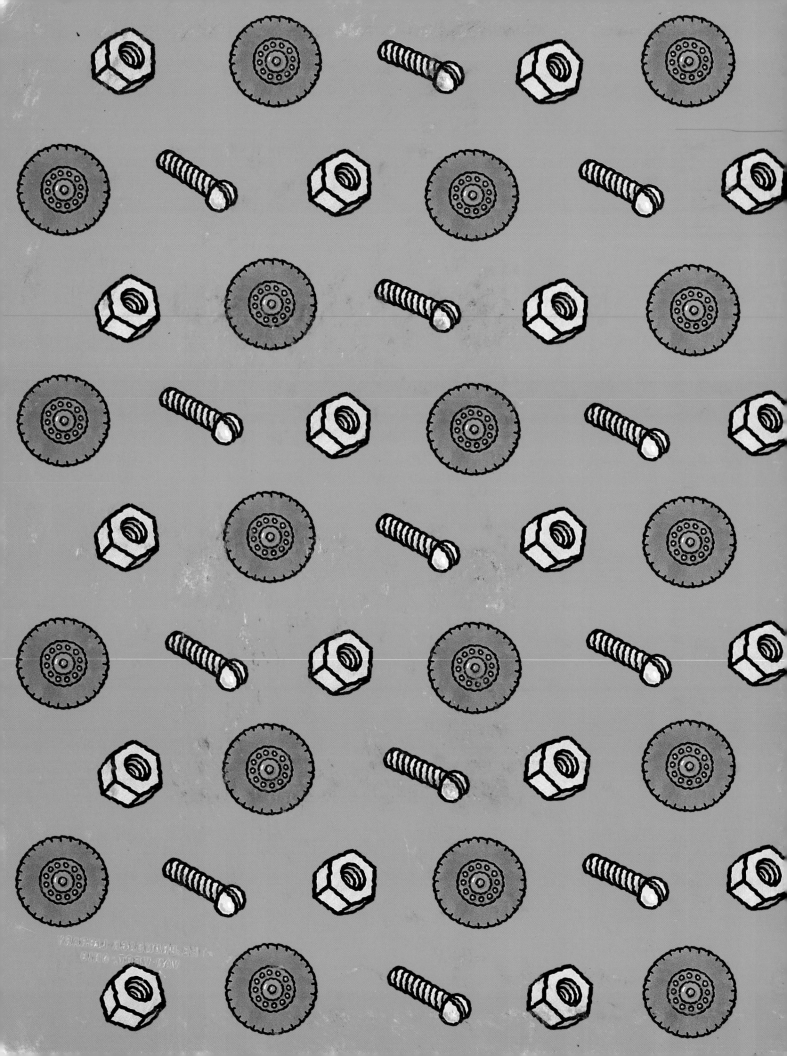